Tudor Jobs

Haydn Middleton

Heinemann
LIBRARY

www.heinemann.co.uk/library
Visit our website to find out more information about **Heinemann Library** books.

To order:
 Phone 44 (0) 1865 888066
 Send a fax to 44 (0) 1865 314091
 Visit the Heinemann Bookshop at www.heinemann.co.uk/library to browse our catalogue and order online.

First published in Great Britain by Heinemann Library, Halley Court, Jordan Hill, Oxford OX2 8EJ, part of Harcourt Education.

Heinemann is a registered trademark of Harcourt Education Ltd.

Editorial: Lucy Thunder and Helen Cox
Design: Jo Hinton-Malivoire, Richard Parker and
    Tinstar Design Limited (www.tinstar.co.uk)
Illustrations: Tokay Interactive Ltd
Picture Research: Rebecca Sodergren
Production: Séverine Ribierre

Originated by Ambassador Litho Ltd
Printed in Hong Kong, China
    by Wing King Tong

ISBN 0 431 14617 9
07 06 05 04 03
10 9 8 7 6 5 4 3 2 1

British Library Cataloguing in Publication Data
Middleton, Haydn
    Tudor Jobs. – (People in the past)
    331.7′00942′09031
A full catalogue record for this book is available from the British Library.

Acknowledgements
The publishers would like to thank the following for permission to reproduce photographs:

AKG pp**8**, **25**; Andy Williams p**23**; Bridgeman Art Library pp**6**, **33**; Christ Church Picture Gallery p**42**; Collections pp**28** (Liz Staves), **34**, **35** (Alain le Garsmeur); Corbis pp**32** (Bettmann) **43**; Donald Cooper/Photostage p**10**; Fotomas Index pp**12**, **22**, **24**, **38**; Glasgow University Library p**15**; Haydn Middleton p**13**; Hulton Getty pp**21**, **29**; John Ryland Library, University of Manchester p**31**; Lambeth Palace Library p**17**; Mary Evans Picture Library pp**20**; **36**, **37**, **41**; Mary Rose Trust/Focal point p**14**; National Portrait Gallery pp**7**, **9**, **11**; Shakespeare Trust p**26**.

Cover photograph of a man chopping wood, from the *Book of Hours*, c.1520, reproduced with permission of Bridgeman Art Library.

The publishers would like to thank Rebecca Vickers for her assistance with the preparation of this book.

Every effort has been made to contact copyright holders of any material reproduced in this book. Any omissions will be rectified in subsequent printings if notice is given to the publishers.

Contents

Words appearing in the text in bold, **like this**, are explained in the Glossary.

The Tudor world

Five hundred years ago the world was a very different place. Europeans were only just realizing that America existed, and they had no idea about Australia. Meanwhile, the mighty **Ottoman Turks** were threatening to conquer the whole of Europe itself. And England (including the Principality of Wales) and Scotland were separate kingdoms, each with its own royal family.

From 1485 to 1603 the Tudor family ruled over England. We now call that period 'Tudor times' and we know the men, women and children who lived then as 'Tudor people'. Some of them were very rich. Many more were extremely poor. In this book you can find out what life was like for both sorts of people.

The Tudor family

The Tudor family ruled England and Wales from 1485 until 1603:

King Henry VII (king from 1485 to 1509)
King Henry VIII (king from 1509 to 1547)
King Edward VI (king from 1547 to 1553)
Queen Mary I (queen from 1553 to 1558)
Queen Elizabeth I (queen from 1558 to 1603)

Jobs for everyone?

The everyday lives of Tudor people – both rich and poor – were not much like ours. Around half the number of children born were dead before their first birthday. Almost everyone believed that God was always watching them, and punishing or rewarding them for the things they did. And most women were closely controlled by their fathers or husbands – they had few, if any, rights of their own. Today we would call them 'second-class **citizens**'.

Most people lived in country villages, not in towns or cities (although there were big cities like London, Bristol and Norwich in Tudor times). The choice and range of jobs – especially for poor people – was much more limited than today.

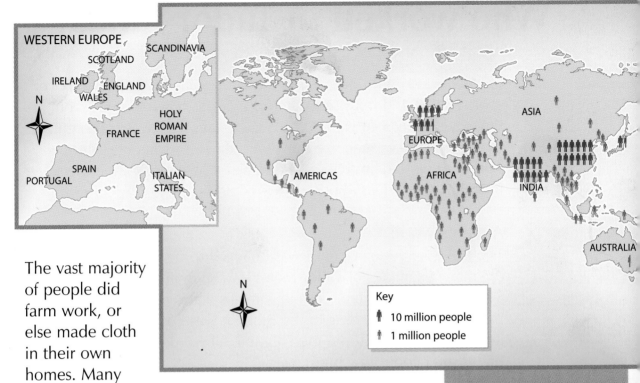

The vast majority of people did farm work, or else made cloth in their own homes. Many boys followed in their fathers' footsteps, doing the same kinds of jobs as them. But by no means everyone could find work.

In spite of so many deaths in early childhood, the Tudor **population** kept on growing. But the number of jobs did not go up too. Meanwhile the **cost of living** kept rising, but people with jobs did not always get wage-rises to match it. This meant that the number of poor people reached record levels. For them, it was often a struggle to survive.

This map gives a rough idea of the size of the world's **population** in early Tudor times. There were far more people living in Europe and Asia than in the rest of the world, and hardly any in America. Europe was split into different countries, some of which are shown here.

Tudor money note

In this book, Tudor sums of money are shown in pounds (£), shillings (s) and pennies (d). There were 12d in a shilling and 20s in a pound – which was worth a lot more then! Most people earned less than £10 in a whole year, and you could go to the theatre for a single penny.

Who worked in Tudor times?

In some ways Tudor people were quite similar to us. They enjoyed sports, fell in and out of love and preferred to live in peace, but at times had to fight in wars. Yet in other ways they were different. From paintings we can see they wore different sorts of clothes. And from written **sources**, we discover that some of their ideas – including their ideas about work – could be very different too.

A man's world

The place for Tudor women was believed to be in the home. There are many examples of Tudor men's low opinion of women. Even Church officials treated women with suspicion and fear. This was partly because according to the Bible, it was Eve who led Adam into sin. Therefore, some men argued, all women should be kept under strict control by men.

There was no such thing as equal job opportunities for men and women. In this book you will read about priests, craftspeople, doctors, actors and writers. Jobs like these were all done by men. Their wives and daughters were often expected to help them with their work. In this man's world, however, women could not lead professional lives of their own.

Most Tudor women spent their working lives in and around the home. These women are preparing food. Very few Tudor pictures show men doing this kind of work!

Two sorts of women

Tudor bishop John Aylmer preached the following words at **court**. 'Women are of two sorts. Some are wiser and more reliable than a number of men. But another and worse sort of them are fond, foolish, … feeble, careless, rash, proud, dainty, tale-bearers, eavesdroppers, rumour-raisers, evil-tongued, worse-minded, and in every way made stupid by the devil.' His view of women was very harsh – even though one of his listeners was Queen Elizabeth I! Many Tudor men, like him, thought most women were not responsible enough to have careers.

For almost half the Tudor period, however, the top job in England was done by a woman. This was the position of **monarch**. Before Tudor times, England was almost always ruled by kings. But first Mary Tudor and then her half-sister Elizabeth reigned as queens. Some men – like the Scot, John Knox – thought rule by women was 'monstriferous'! But Elizabeth, who reigned from 1558 until 1603, proved to be an excellent monarch.

Queen Elizabeth I showed that England's top job could be done by a woman as well as by men. 'I know I have the body of a weak and feeble woman,' she once said in a speech, 'but I have the heart and stomach of a king, and of a king of England too.'

Servant

Today we think of houses being lived in by families. Many Tudor homes were lived in not just by families but by their male and female servants as well. (Being a servant was one of the few jobs that plenty of women and girls were allowed to do.) These servants did jobs ranging from cooking and dairy-maiding to laundry work. Even some quite poor families might have a single maid.

In the household

All the people who lived under one roof were known as the 'household'. Each person had to obey and respect the master of the household. In return, the master looked after them all in an almost fatherly way.

Some young servants were **apprentices**. Usually they were boys, and their masters made them sign a contract called an 'indenture'. This described their pay and what their duties would be over a period of up to ten years. For example, a tailor's apprentice might have to sew together the seams of cloth cut by the tailor. Some apprentices received only 'bed and board'. This meant they shared the family meal and were given a place in the house to sleep.

This 16th century painting shows a servant is pouring wine for customers at a town inn. If town servants were unhappy in their work, they had more chances to find new jobs than servants who worked in remote places in the countryside.

CARDINAL WOLSEY

Thomas Wolsey was a Tudor success story until he fell out with the king he served, Henry VIII. Wolsey went from butcher's son to Lord Chancellor.

Royal servants

The richer a family was, the more servants it usually had. The royal family had most of all. The Tudor **monarchs** employed over 2000 paid servants. Some royal servants helped govern the kingdom as well as serving the monarch.

Unlike today, men did not have to go through examinations or interviews to get such jobs. Instead they tried to win the **patronage** or support of a leading **courtier**. He might then recommend that the monarch employ them.

Inheriting jobs

A high-ranking royal servant might even pass on his job to his son or to another relative when he retired. This meant the best-qualified men did not always get the jobs they deserved. In Tudor times, the best way to get ahead was to get yourself a very good **patron**.

The King's devoted servant

Men from poor backgrounds could rise high by serving the monarch. Thomas Wolsey (c.1472–1530) began life as the son of a butcher in Ipswich. He took jobs in the Church and in 1507 was promoted to royal **chaplain**. King Henry VIII came to rely on him. By 1518 Cardinal Wolsey was both Archbishop of York and Lord Chancellor of England. To some people, he seemed richer, grander and possibly even more powerful than the king. Then in 1529 Henry decided he no longer needed him. For the 'Butcher's Boy' the fairytale was over. He fell from power as fast as he had risen.

Local official

The Tudor **monarchs** could not govern England and Wales all by themselves. At their **court** in London, they were helped by many **courtiers** and officials. They also worked with members of **Parliament**, who came to London from all around the kingdom to advise the monarch and to pass laws.

Law enforcers

Who made sure that everyone in the kingdom – from Cornwall in the south to the Scottish borders in the north – obeyed these laws? Specially-trained men called **assize** judges took travelling law-courts around the kingdom. In certain 'assize towns' they sat and heard important **legal** cases.

Quite wealthy local men called **Justices of the Peace** (or JPs) also held courts, called **Quarter Sessions**. In 1580, there were nearly 2000 of them throughout the kingdom's counties. Usually JPs had no legal training. They had to make sure roads were repaired and hedges were put up, as well as bringing criminals to justice.

The plays of William Shakespeare (1564–1616) are a wonderful **source** of information about life in Tudor England. Here, in *Much Ado About Nothing*, we see Constable Dogberry instructing some town watchmen before they make their regular night patrol.

Crime in Tudor England

Detecting crime was not easy, since there was no police force in Tudor England. Men called constables were elected by local **parish** officials for a year at a time. Their duties included keeping up the local stock of weapons and armour, and collecting **taxes**. They were also supposed to track down criminals. Often, however, the victims of crime had to do this themselves.

What kind of crimes were they? At courts in Essex between 1559 and 1603, there were 3129 cases. Out of these, 60 per cent were for theft, 10 per cent for burglary, 3.5 per cent for highway robbery, 5 per cent for killing people and 5.5 per cent for witchcraft!

Sir Roger Manwood (1525–92), a judge. Officials like him dealt with cases that were too tough for JPs, who were usually unpaid.

A constable's oath

A new constable in a parish had to take this oath: 'You shall arrest all persons who carry threatening weapons or disturb the peace … You shall make sure that watchmen in your town catch **vagabonds**, night-walkers, eavesdroppers, spies … and that murderers, thieves and other criminals are tracked down … You shall bring to court anyone breaking the laws against drinking too much in inns and alehouses …' We cannot be sure how many of these duties he carried out successfully.

Priest

'Everyone in this realm … shall, if they have no lawful or reasonable excuse to be absent, go to their **parish** church or chapel every Sunday, and on other holy days, and behave themselves in an orderly way during the service …'

That comes from a law of 1559. Anyone who did not attend church, or misbehaved while there, could be fined 12d – and the money could be used to help the parish poor.

Today people are free to choose to follow any religion or not be religious at all. In the 1500s, people *had* to go to church, and they *had* to follow only one religion. In England after 1558 this was the **Protestant** faith. Tudor politician William Cecil wrote that no two religions could ever be allowed in a single country – for people argued and fought about religion more than anything else.

Changes in the Church

The English people had to follow the faith of their Tudor **monarchs**. Henry VIII stopped everyone from obeying the **Catholic Pope** in Rome. Mary I made everyone go back to being Catholic again.

A page from the *Book of Martyrs* by Tudor priest John Foxe who became the vicar of Shipton. Translated from Latin into English in 1563, it described cruel treatments of Protestants by Catholics. By law, copies were placed in every Protestant English cathedral and in many parish churches.

When Elizabeth I became monarch, she ruled that England's religion should be Protestant again! This must have been confusing for many people in the kingdom's 9,000 parishes. It was confusing for parish priests too.

Priests were meant to be 'honest, sober and wise men, who can read the scriptures well to the people'. They also held services for **christenings**, marriages and funerals, made sure records were kept of these events, and helped local people with any writing they might have to do. Priests were not always highly educated. In some parishes the priest's pay was no higher than that of a farm labourer. The pay rose in later Tudor times.

At this parish church at Morebath in Devon, a man served as a priest from 1520 to 1574. Few Tudors lived or worked this long!

Doctor and surgeon

Tudor people did not keep themselves as clean as we do. Nor did they know much about germs. So they caught many fatal diseases, including the dreaded plague. There were few qualified doctors, and even their knowledge was not very good. When plague broke out, they could only try to stop the disease from spreading. But in a single outbreak of plague in 1563, one person out of every four or five died in London alone.

Since there was no free **National Health Service**, local doctors had to be paid for their work. They might demand a fee of £1 per day. Poor people could hardly ever afford this. So, if they lived in towns, they went instead for advice to an 'apothecary'. He was a shopkeeper who sold herbs, spices and medicines.

Many doctors today work in hospitals; so do surgeons. In Tudor times there were no hospitals like ours. But sometimes barbers also did surgeons' work, and performed operations on their customers. Nor were there any **antiseptics**. This meant that even if the limb was chopped off successfully, the stump might then get infected by germs and the patient might still die.

These items from a barber-surgeon's kit were found on board a Tudor ship, the *Mary Rose*. A wooden mallet was with them. Maybe the surgeon on board used it for knocking out his patients before operating on them!

Doctor John Hall

John Hall, the son of a doctor, studied at Cambridge University. Around 1600 he started to work as a doctor in Stratford-upon-Avon. He won a good reputation for treating diseases ranging from measles to **melancholy**. He kept a record of his cases and the cures that he tried out. For a boy who wetted the bed, he gave a powder made from the windpipe of a cockerel. He also made 'Scorbutick Beer' from herbs and roots for a disease called scurvy. Victims caught it through not getting enough Vitamin C from fruit and vegetables. Then their gums swelled up and bled, and old wounds elsewhere on their bodies might open up and bleed too.

How to cut off a leg

This description for cutting off a leg comes from a Tudor handbook 'for all young surgeons', published in 1591:

'Put the patient on a good, strong, steady bench. A man behind him must hold him tight by both his arms ... Another strong man must hold the leg tightly above the place where it is to be sawn off. He should have a large hand and a good grip, to help to stop the bleeding.'

There is no mention of any **anaesthetic**. Patients had to make do with strong drink to dull the pain – or maybe they were just knocked out (see picture on page 14).

This leading surgeon would not have worked in a barber's shop. Here he is lecturing to students on the workings of the human body.

Cunning man or woman

'A great many of us, when we are in trouble, or sick, or lose anything, we run hither and thither to witches and wise men … and ask them to help us.' Bishop Hugh Latimer said that in 1552. By the end of the century, several writers noted that there was a so-called 'cunning man or woman' in every village – and that many people went to them to sort out their problems.

People who put things right

The old word 'cunning' just meant 'knowing'. Most cunning men or women had no training. They just 'knew' how to put things right in a world where a lot went wrong. They could use good or 'white' magic to lift spells, identify local thieves, tell the future or forecast the weather to anxious farmers. People paid them small fees for their services. But usually cunning men did other jobs too. They might, for example, be millers or shoemakers.

Church officials disliked what they called their 'unholy' magic. There were laws against some of their activities. But all kinds of people kept turning to them for help. In 1583–84, the cloth was stolen from the **communion** table in a Berkshire church. The church officials called in the local cunning woman to find the thief.

Tudor people had a far greater belief in magic than we do. **Monarchs** were supposed to be able to cure a disease called scrofula by touching the victim's skin. Each one of England's Tudor rulers held ceremonies where they tried this out. But people believed in black as well as white magic. Sometimes they blamed 'servants of the devil' for *causing* diseases or disasters. This was impossible to prove. Even so, 'witches' were executed after tests and trials. There was a law against being a witch until 1736.

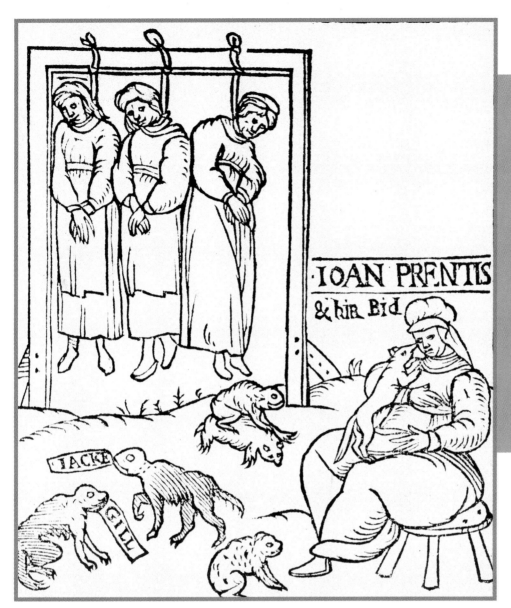

IOAN PRENTIS
& his Bid

JACKE

GILL

These three 'witches' were hanged in Chelmsford, Essex, in 1589. The creatures at their feet were supposed to contain 'evil spirits', sent by the devil to help them do their bad deeds. Evil spirits could be disguised as cats, dogs, rats, toads, wasps or even butterflies – or so people thought!

Goodwife Veazy's cure for worms

If a person was suffering from worms, a cunning woman known as Goodwife Veazy had a cure. She said three times, 'In the name of God I begin and in the name of God I do end. Thou worm be gone from hence in the name of the Father, of the Son, and of the Holy Ghost.' Then she spread a little honey and pepper on the part of the person's body that was affected. She must have been successful, because in 1604 she was recommended to a leading politician! Other prayers of this kind were not said but written on a piece of paper, then hung around the sufferer's neck.

Farmer

'Whoever does not maintain the plough destroys this kingdom.'
That was the opinion of Elizabeth I's chief minister, Lord Burghley.
He meant that without farming, England could not have survived.

Nine out of every ten Tudor people lived in the countryside. Most of them did farmwork of some kind. These people produced the raw materials, like corn and wool, that fed and clothed the nation. What they farmed depended on the quality of the soil, the weather and on each farmer's own choice.

The yearly round

Some men farmed on a big scale. Others produced only enough to supply their own families. But through the seasons of each year, they all worked the same long hours – using simple tools like hoes, wooden ploughs and **scythes,** and without today's machines to speed things up.

In spring they ploughed and **sowed** oats, wheat and barley, put their animals out to grass and sheared their sheep. In summer they ploughed again and made hay.

mixed farming types

pasture farming types (open land)

pasture farming types (wooded land)

NORTHUMBERLAND

DURHAM

CUMBERLAND

WESTMORLAND

LANCASHIRE

YORKSHIRE

● York

N

LINCOLNSHIRE

CHESHIRE

DERBYSHIRE

NOTTING-HAMSHIRE

STAFFORDSHIRE

LEICESTERSHIRE

CAMBRIDGESHIRE

NORFOLK

SHROPSHIRE

NORTHAMPTONSHIRE

WARWICK-SHIRE

BEDFORDSHIRE

SUFFOLK

HEREFORDSHIRE

WORCESTERSHIRE

HERTFORDSHIRE

ESSEX

BUCKINGHAMSHIRE

GLOUCESTERSHIRE

OXFORDSHIRE

BERKSHIRE

London
●

WILTSHIRE

SURREY

KENT

SOMERSET

HAMPSHIRE

SUSSEX

DEVON

DORSET

CORNWALL

The main kinds of farming that people did in Tudor England. Since the **population** was growing so fast, farmers had to meet an ever-increasing demand for food and drink and wool and animal hides.

In late summer they harvested their grain crops and let their animals graze on the stubble. During the autumn they picked fruit, sowed winter wheat and barley, **threshed** grain and made sure there was enough winter fodder to feed their animals. Early in winter they killed any pigs and cows that could not be fed until spring. Then during the winter months they mended tools, buildings, fences, barns and hedges and looked after lambs and calves that were born early.

Crop developments

Towards the end of Tudor times, some farmers began to grow new crops. In the south a yellow-flowered plant, called woad, was grown to make blue dye for cloth. By 1586 around 20,000 people spent part of each year growing it. Tobacco was first sown in 1571. Carrots were being grown in fields by 1597. And coleseed or 'rape' became important as sheep-food and as a source of oil.

A farmer's goods

We can tell from the **inventories** of Tudor farmers what kinds of farming they did. Around 1560 Simon Austrey farmed Provender Farm. This was what he left behind when he died:

wheat (in barns)	£14 13s
peas and hay (in barns)	£3 6s 2d
oats (in barns)	£2 14s
barley	£5
8 horses, harnesses etc.	£23
cows and calves	£14 7s 2d
38 acres of wheat	£32
6 acres of oats	£2
17 acres of peas	£13 6s 8d
24 acres of barley	£11 4s
29 pigs	£4 5s
ewes and lambs	£22 5s 4d
poultry	16s 4d
tools and carts	£4 5s
TOTAL WORTH	**£163 2s 6d**

Farm labourer

Not everyone who did farmwork ran his own farm. During Tudor times, the number of farm labourers (workers) grew and grew. Some of them were called 'servants of **husbandry**'. These were young, unmarried men and women who lived in the household of a farmer who employed them and paid them low wages. Often labourers moved from farm to farm, saving what money they could. By the age of 25, most of them had married and become 'day-labourers'. They then lived in their own simple homes, and worked for richer farmers when work was available.

Labourers had to do all kinds of farm jobs – like mending walls, tending orchards, shearing sheep, planting and harvesting. In the 1590s an unskilled day-labourer might work for 312 days a year, earning about 9d a day. Skilled jobs were better paid; hired ploughmen received 1s 2d a day. While the **cost of living** kept rising, however, it could still be very hard to get by.

Sheep everywhere
The number of sheep grew in Tudor times. There was a huge demand for wool, to make cloth (see page 27). Therefore more and more Tudor farmers turned from growing crops to keeping sheep. An example of this was the Spencer family of Althorp in Northamptonshire, who became big sheep-farmers.

A Tudor farm labourer planting a stake for climbing plants. Farm tools had hardly changed in hundreds of years. There were plenty of new books on how to farm more efficiently, but very few men could read them.

By later Tudor times, they had a flock of 14,000 sheep and lambs – and they made a fortune from selling the wool and **mutton**. (Four centuries later, a Spencer from Althorp married into the royal family and became Diana, Princess of Wales.)

A lone shepherd tends his flock. He might let the sheep graze on the hills during the day. He would then pen them in on **arable** downland at night, so that their droppings **fertilized** the ground for growing crops.

Farmers like the Spencers needed far fewer labourers to look after sheep than for other sorts of farming. Some labourers were employed as shepherds, but many more lost their jobs and homes.

Tips on lamb-shearing

'Let lambs go unclipped, till June be half worn,
The better their fleeces will grow to be shorn.'

That farming tip is one of many given in *Five Hundred Points of Good Husbandry*, written by Thomas Tusser (c.1515–1580). He went on: 'If they are shorn [with shears] while the nights are cold, they will get stiff, and not be able to rise in the mornings … But if you leave the wool on too long, it gets hard for the creature to eat or move. Then its wool will get matted and not be worth anything.' He also advised shepherds to keep their animals off paths and roads, since sandy wool was harder to cut.

Housewife

'Rise early and sweep the house. Then milk the cows, feed the calves and take the milk to the dairy. Wake and dress the children and make breakfast also for your husband, the children and the servants and eat with them. Then you should make sure corn and malt have gone to the mill, and bake and brew what is needed.'

That advice to a farmer's wife comes from Anthony Fitzherbert's *Book of **Husbandry***, first printed in 1523. When a woman today says she is 'just a housewife', it usually means she does all sorts of unpaid jobs in and around the house. Tudor housewives were constantly active too – whether or not they had servants. Other jobs they might do regularly included making cheese and butter, and feeding kept animals like pigs and chickens. Also, if their husbands kept sheep, they made clothes from the wool.

Many Tudor housewives earned extra money by turning wool into cloth. This home-based **industry** was called 'the domestic system'. There were no factories like we have today.

Tudor housewives went to markets in nearby towns like this one – modern-day Burford in Oxfordshire – where there was a weekly market for wool, cloth and corn. The women sold and bought any extra goods. Going to market was a social occasion.

Alewives

During busy periods like harvest-time, country housewives were expected to work with the menfolk in the fields. At home, they might bring in extra pennies by setting up an alehouse. The 'alewife' as she was known would sell ale, beer and cider, which she might have brewed herself. The government tried to limit the number of alehouses. By 1577, however, there were around 15,000 of them across the country. Tudor people liked their alcohol!

A lady of leisure

Not all Tudor housewives were frantically busy. The quote below is from the diary of the wealthy **Puritan** Lady Margaret Hoby. Religion played a huge part in her life: 'In the morning after praying and ordering dinner I wrote some notes in my Bible till 10 o'clock. Then I went for a walk and, prayed, read a chapter of the Bible, and embroidered. After dinner I embroidered and did some things about the house till 4. Then I wrote into my book the sermon from yesterday … gave order for supper, and prayed.'

Miner

Some people who lived in the countryside did not just do farmwork. In Cornwall they dug tin from ancient mines. In north-eastern and midland England, and in south Wales, they dug coal from fields. Meanwhile in Derbyshire and the Mendip Hills they mined larger and larger amounts of lead. And in the Weald (an area stretching across Sussex, Surrey and Kent), they dug out and **smelted** 12,000 tonnes of **iron ore** in 1600 alone.

Part-timers and professionals

Sometimes families paid a landowner for the right to mine iron, coal or stone on his or her land. Some landowners ran the mines themselves and paid miners to do the digging. These miners might just be part-timers, who also did farm jobs. Or they could be full-time professionals, like the lead miners of the Mendip Hills.

'A doubtful and dangerous occupation'

Coal mining has always been a tough job. Even in the 20th century many miners died in accidents and disasters.

Few Tudor pictures show people working at **industrial** jobs, partly because artists were not interested in showing them. This picture, from around 1566, shows mine-workers producing salt. Salt was used to **preserve** meat.

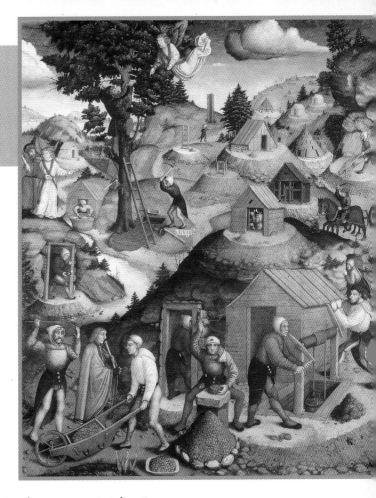

A law from mid-Tudor times called mining 'a doubtful and dangerous occupation'. Up to a hundred men could work in the same mine. For safety reasons they had to work closely together in teams, make sure they all did everything on time, and watch out for one another. But in the cramped mines, men could still die if tunnels collapsed on them, if fires broke out, or if they fell into underground streams.

Not all industrial work took place in the countryside. Some newer high-quality goods were made in towns, for wealthy customers to buy. The best steel knives, for example, were made in Sheffield. Cheaper ones were produced in the surrounding villages.

Down the mine

Some Tudor mine-owners' **accounts** have survived. They tell us what kinds of jobs miners had to do. First coal-cutters using picks dug out the coal by the light of candles. Then different men collected up the cut coal, and wheeled it in barrows to a third group, called 'bankmen'. The bankmen hoisted the coal to the surface, using pulleys, then stacked it up. None of these jobs was very well paid. And if a miner died underground, his workmates had to pay to have his body brought up – only to bury it again, this time in a Christian grave!

Craftsperson

One Tudor person in every ten lived in a city or town. Many of them worked in the craft **industries** and traded with one another. You may know someone today with the surname Smith, Taylor, Weaver, Fuller, Skinner, Baker, Carpenter or Wright. Such names might tell you what jobs their ancestors used to do.

This photo shows what a Tudor glovemaker's workshop would have looked like. John Shakespeare, the father of the famous playwright, William Shakespeare (see page 32), was a glover and a skinner.

You can easily guess what (black)smiths, tailors, weavers, bakers and carpenters did. Fullers cleansed and thickened cloth. Skinners stripped the skins from animals, and made them ready to be turned into clothes. 'Wright' was an old word for a maker or builder.

Working from dawn to dusk

In 1563, **Parliament** passed a law that laid down what hours people should work. The Tudor working day seems very long to us today. But we cannot be sure if all employers made their workers obey this law: 'All labourers being hired for wages on a daily or weekly basis shall between March and September be at their work at or before 5 am, and continue at work until between 7 and 8 pm – except in the time of breakfast, dinner or drinking (not more than two and a half hours in each day).'

Town craftsmen usually worked in their own homes but belonged to a 'guild'. These organizations laid down rules on standards of workmanship, decided what finished goods should cost and set wages. They also made sure **apprentices** were properly trained by their masters – for up to as long as ten years. The guilds also looked after any craftsmen who had fallen on hard times.

England's biggest industry

More people worked at making woollen cloth than in any other industry. The finished cloth was used to make clothes, and plenty was left to be **exported**. More and more cloth was made in later Tudor times, especially after foreign cloth-workers came from the Netherlands to settle in Kent and East Anglia.

Some woollen cloth was made in towns like Worcester and Shrewsbury. But country-dwellers made most of it in their own homes. Children and women usually **carded** the wool and spun it using a spinning wheel or distaff. Then the men wove it into cloth on machines called looms. Families got the raw wool and the looms from a **merchant** called a 'putter-out'. When they had finished their work, he took away what they had made, then sold it. This 'putting-out' system was used in other trades too: tailoring, shoemaking and cabinet-making in London; **hosiery** in Leicester; and nail-making in Staffordshire and the West Midlands.

Merchant

'London is a large, excellent and mighty city of business …,' wrote Jacob Rathgeb, a German visitor in 1592. 'Many of the inhabitants are employed in buying and selling **merchandise** and trading in almost every corner of the world.'

Such people – known as **merchants** – existed in busy cities like Bristol, Exeter and Newcastle too. They bought goods cheaply in one place then sold them, for more money, in another. From their profits they could grow very wealthy. Some became so rich, they were able to lend money to the government. Others, like Sir Andrew Judd and Sir Thomas White, became Lord Mayors of London.

Branching out overseas

English merchants used sailing ships to send abroad items such as tin, lead, animal skins and fish. But the richest **export** trade by far was in cloth woven from wool. Overseas people bought it in great amounts to make clothes with. By 1600 this trade was worth £750,000 per year. It was run mainly by a London-based organization called the Merchant Adventurers.

Many Tudor merchants built attractive glass-windowed houses for themselves and their families. This fine house, at Coggeshall in Essex, is still standing today.

Luxuries from abroad

English merchants imported luxury goods for the rich from all over the known world. The most important of these was French wine. But surviving Tudor records from 1558 to 1604 list some more surprising items too: tennis balls, bought in sets of 1000; little bone picks for getting wax out of people's ears, which came in sets of 144 (a dozen dozens); and live bears from northern Europe. These were used for the popular 'sport' of bear-baiting – making dogs attack a chained-up bear.

Merchants exported the cloth in the form of 'broadcloths'. These were bundles of fabric each over 25 metres long, more than 1.5 metres wide and weighing at least 29 kilograms. Wool had to be clipped from 50 to 60 sheep to make just one of them! By the mid-1500s, English merchants were exporting about 130,000 broadcloths each year.

In earlier Tudor times, most English cloths were sent a short sea journey away to Antwerp, which was then in the Netherlands (now part of Belgium). From there, foreign merchants took the cloth to many parts of Europe. In later times, English merchants began to trade directly with places as distant as Russia, Morocco and even eastern Asia. Some of these places had warm climates, where lighter clothing was needed. So English merchants produced new forms of cloth, mixing wool and **worsted**. By 1600 the new cloth was selling for £250,000 per year.

The German merchants in this picture from 1518 are working out their **accounts**. They had no computers to help them!

Printer

There were handwritten books in England for at least 1000 years before Tudor times. But England's first printed book was made in 1477. It was a collection of the sayings of brilliant men, made at Westminster by William Caxton. Caxton had learned how to print books in Europe, where modern publishing had just begun.

Tudor England had fewer printers and printing **presses** than several other European countries. London was the centre of the English **industry**. By law, only the university towns of Oxford and Cambridge were also allowed to have presses. England's rulers wanted to control what books were published because new ideas – especially about religion – could cause trouble. In 1538, the government even tried to keep all foreign printed books out of the country.

What did people read?

It is hard to know how many Tudor people could actually read. Historians try to find out by looking at the number of people who were unable to sign their names on documents. (If they could not read, they probably could not write either.) In 1600, 72 per cent of men and 92 per cent of women were not even able to write their signatures. Most of them had little use for books – whether printed or handwritten.

Dr Dee's library

As more books were printed, more libraries were built to keep them in. The famous scientist and **astrologer** John Dee (1527–1608) built up a vast library at Mortlake, near London. In 1575 Queen Elizabeth I and her leading ministers visited him, to inspect his 3000 printed books and 500 manuscripts. His house had a less welcome visit in 1583, after Dee left for a trip abroad. A crowd of people broke in and destroyed much of his library and furniture. They feared his books were full of dangerous magic.

If it plese ony man spirituel or temporel to bye ony pyes of two and thre comemoraciōs of salisburi vse enpryntid after the forme of this preset lettre whiche ben wel and truly correct, late hym come to westmonester in to the almonesrye at the reed pale and he shal haue them good chepe ...

Supplico stet cedula

Pray, do not pull down the Advertisemen

A printed advert from the late 15th century. Printer William Caxton invites 'any man' to visit his press at Westminster, and there he will find books 'good cheap'.

Tudor printers did not make much money. They had to pay specialist workers high wages to arrange the metal letters, to put ink on the **type**, and then squeeze the inked type and paper together in the press. Then someone would need to bring all the pages together and bind them as a book.

England's main printing-houses produced law books, text books for schools and universities and many religious works – some illustrated, some not. New printers started up businesses too, publishing books of 'jests' (jokes), pamphlets (small booklets) and plays. One printer, Robert Wyer, made good profits by producing small, cheap books giving information on the weather, the care of horses, the treatment of illnesses and **horoscopes**.

Writer

Today in Britain more than 50,000 different books are published each year. In early Tudor times, there were only about 800 books each decade (ten years). In the last ten years of Tudor times, that number rose to nearly 3000. They included books about religion, long poems and little books of **horoscopes**. As more people learned to read, there was a greater demand for books – and for writers.

In early Tudor times, writers wrote mainly in Latin and Greek. They did not believe English was a true 'language of learning'. But after William Tyndale translated the Bible into English in the 1520s, more and more writers used English. They wrote more and more about England too. Books and plays on English history were very popular. Many Tudor people learned a lot about old English kings like Henry V and Richard III from William Shakespeare's plays. Sometimes, however, Shakespeare twisted the facts a little to make his plots more exciting!

Perhaps the greatest English writer: William Shakespeare (1564–1616). He wrote such famous plays as *Romeo and Juliet*, *Hamlet* and *Macbeth*. He was the son of a glovemaker, and he acted and directed plays as well as writing. Although many of his plays are set abroad, he may never have left England to research them.

People's wills and **inventories** show us that more and more people were taking an interest in books. In 1560 in Canterbury, Kent, only eight per cent of inventories had books in them. By the 1620s, 45 per cent recorded books – like this illustrated 'Book of Hours' from around 1500.

Books in print

Not all Tudor writers wanted their work to be printed in books. The poet John Donne said it was 'ungentlemanly' to have poetry printed. So during his lifetime his friends just passed around hand-written copies of his poems. Shakespeare too was dead before all his plays appeared in print. But many people already knew his plays well, from seeing them performed on stage.

Tudor writers relied on rich **patrons** to keep them going. These patrons gave them financial help or found them day jobs to do. In return, the writers gave them glory by **dedicating** their works to them – usually in a very flattering way.

John Donne loses his day job

In 1597, John Donne became secretary to Lord Egerton, a top politician. With Egerton as his patron, he wrote a lot of wonderful poetry that people still read today. But then he fell in love with one of Egerton's young relatives and secretly married her. Donne was 29 and the girl, Anne More, was only 16. Egerton was furious and refused to employ and support him any more. 'I need an occupation,' Donne wrote in despair, before taking up a successful career as a priest.

Architect and builder

Most Tudor houses were not built to last. Many labourers' homes were flimsy one-room cottages put up in a single night on heath or woodland. In 1602 Richard Carew described homes in Cornwall having 'walls of earth, low thatched roofs, few partitions [inside walls], no floorboards or glass windows, and scarcely any chimneys other than a hole in the wall to let out smoke.' Such buildings did not need an expert to design them.

Designing and building

Most **monarchs** and **courtiers** had little interest in ideas about **architecture**. (Only one book was published on the subject in the whole of Elizabeth I's reign.) Rich people usually decided for themselves how they wanted their grand new building to look, then they asked an architect to draw up a 'platt' or plan for the builders to follow. Sometimes the architect also supervised the building teams; sometimes the owner did it. Only 'gentlemen', it was believed, had the taste and brains to create grand houses. Yet the creator of Chatsworth House and Hardwick Hall was not a man at all but a woman – Elizabeth Hardwick, Countess of Shrewsbury, born in 1521 (see the box opposite).

Large brick-built houses, like this one at Compton Wynyates, in Warwickshire became more common in Tudor times. In some counties, brick was used for buildings in small towns too.

Longleat House, which still stands today, was built by Sir John Thynne in the late 1560s. Elegant country houses like this were very different from the homes of the rich in the Middle Ages. In those more violent times, wealthy people lived in castles to protect themselves and their possessions.

England's first true architect?

Robert Smythson (c.1536–1614) was one of the first Englishmen actually to be called an architect. On his tombstone, it says that he was the architect of several great buildings, including Wollaton Hall, near Nottingham.

Smythson helped Sir Francis Willoughby to design Wollaton Hall – built high on a hill, so that it could be seen for miles around. Smythson and Willoughby were very impressed by new architectural styles in Europe. So parts of Wollaton Hall ended up looking Italian, French and **Flemish**.

Building Hardwick Hall

Robert Smythson drew up the plan for the Countess of Shrewsbury's new home, Hardwick Hall in Derbyshire. But she then kept a sharp eye on the team that put the house together. Surviving **accounts** show it took about seven years to build. Labourers were paid 6d a day, on average, plus basic food like milk, oatmeal and herrings. As the house went up, they probably spent the nights inside its walls. Women sometimes did lighter jobs – polishing stone, carrying water to the men and collecting up rubbish. When the work was finished, four musicians played the Countess into her new home.

Actor

Paul Hentzner, a German, made a record of his visit to London in 1598. He found there several theatres where actors put on shows to very big audiences. These shows ended – he wrote – with music, dancing and wild applause. The next year Thomas Platter from Switzerland noted: 'Every day around two in the afternoon in London two and sometimes even three plays are performed at different places, in order to make people merry.'

Tudor people clearly loved to be entertained by actors. Yet theatres were quite new things.

Actors come off the road

Before late-Tudor times, groups of actors called 'companies' toured England's towns and cities. They performed in market squares or inn yards. Life on the roads of England could be dangerous and uncomfortable, so the actors deserved money that they collected after their shows. The first specially-built, fixed-place theatre was probably London's Red Lion in 1567. The Swan, a later theatre, held up to 3000 people – the rich sitting in expensive seats, the poor standing up after paying just a penny to get in. They were able to watch plays by fine new writers like Thomas Kyd, Christopher Marlowe and William Shakespeare.

A Dutch visitor drew this picture of the Swan theatre, London, in 1596. Actors usually performed in front of no scenery and under open roofs. Cannonballs were rolled around to make the sound of thunder.

Shakespeare belonged to a company called the Lord Chamberlain's Men, based at The Globe theatre in London. He acted as well as wrote. But to Tudor audiences he was not as famous as Richard Burbage or Will Kempe – actors who starred in the first productions of some of his plays. Shakespeare, Burbage and Kempe also helped to pay for the plays to be put on. In return, they took a share of the money the audience paid to get in. Actors who became 'sharers' in this way could earn good money. Shakespeare made about £200 a year in the 1590s. That was ten times what a well-paid schoolmaster could earn.

Will Kempe (right) was one of Tudor London's most popular comic actors and dancers. He was probably the first actor to play the character Bottom in Shakespeare's famous play, *A Midsummer Night's Dream*.

Soldier

In 1554 an **ambassador** from Venice made a report on England's soldiers. There were about 15,000 knights, he wrote, who fought on horseback with spears and swords. Then there were about 85,000 soldiers who fought on foot.

Soldiers fell into four groups. The first and most important were archers who fought with bows and arrows. Second were **infantrymen** who carried weapons called 'billhooks' – poles with curved blades at the end, often used for pruning tree branches.

Third were men who fired a long gun called an 'arquebus'. Last were men who fought with 'pikes' – a pole with a pointed iron or steel tip that could be thrust at a horse carrying a knight.

This picture shows a 16th-century soldier, dressed as was usual – neither in a uniform nor in armour. His only weapon is his sword.

Defending the Nation

Today professional soldiers and sailors defend Britain in times of emergency. There were no such 'regular' soldiers in Tudor times. Henry VII and Henry VIII relied on English **noblemen** to serve as their generals, and also to provide them with soldiers.

In 1513 Henry VIII led a huge force of 35,000 men to try to conquer France. He failed, and in later Tudor times soldiers were needed more often for defence than attack. From 1585 to 1604, **Protestant** England was at war with mighty **Catholic** Spain. A 'militia' or home guard of trained soldiers had to be ready if the Spanish invaded.

An old law said that all able-bodied men between the ages of 16 and 60 must 'bear arms for their **monarch**', if needed. This meant they were expected to practise archery in case they ever had to fight. But by later Tudor times, soldiers also had to know how to fight with pikes and guns too. So, from 1573, small bands from each county were chosen for special training. By 1588, 26,000 men had been trained up. These part-time soldiers formed the core of each county's defence force. But they never saw any real fighting. The Spanish *did* send a great fleet or 'Armada', in 1588. But the English navy drove it off before it could put any soldiers ashore.

English soldiers overseas

Elizabeth I sent small armies to help the Protestants of the Netherlands fight their Catholic Spanish enemies. Some English gentlemen fought as paid volunteers for the *other* side too. They were Catholics who cared more for their religion than their country. Spanish records from 1595 named one English soldier serving the King of Spain as 'Guido Fauques' – or Guy Fawkes. Ten years later, Fawkes took part in the Gunpowder Plot to blow up James I, the king who ruled England after Elizabeth.

Pedlar

Most poor Tudor people seldom travelled far from their homes. But some took to the roads to try to earn extra pennies. A few were tinkers who mended household objects. A few were entertainers who performed 'magic' tricks, juggled or played music. Others were travelling actors or fortune tellers.

Then there were pedlars, who walked from place to place 'peddling' or selling goods that might be found in corner shops today. People also called them 'swigmen' or 'swadders'. Women who followed this trade were known as 'bawdy baskets'.

On the wrong side of the law

Pedlars sometimes carried cheap printed ballads (songs). These could be funny, gory or romantic, telling tales of singing fish or betrayed lovers. Other pedlars, known as 'Irish toyles', carried small things like lace and pins. They timed their visits to houses when only servants or children were at home. Then they tricked them into taking a pennyworth of lace and paying for it with wool or grain that was ten times more valuable.

A pedlar's wares

'Gloves as sweet as damask roses,
Masks for faces and for noses;
Bugle-bracelet, necklace-amber,
Perfume for a lady's chamber;
Golden quoifs [headscarves] and stomachers
For my lads to give their dears;
Pins and poking-sticks of steel;
What maids lack from head to heel!
Come buy of me, come, come buy, come buy,
Buy lads, or else your lasses cry; come buy!'

That was the cry of Autolycus the pedlar in William Shakespeare's play, *A Winter's Tale*. Although he was selling luxury items for women, he was appealing to men who had money to buy them!

This upmarket pedlar, drawn around the start of Tudor times, is selling glass items. Glass was very expensive, so he probably looked only for rich customers.

Village people treated pedlars and tinkers with suspicion. Tinkers went into homes to mend pots and pans. That gave dishonest ones – or their female travelling companions – a chance to steal other things at the same time. Some dishonest pedlars helped themselves to sheets that housewives had laid out on hedges to dry; others picked pockets. If caught, they could be beaten or hanged. But with no police force to arrest them, many went free.

Pedlars were also attracted to local fairs. These were not just places to have fun, as they are today. Tudor fairs were like job-centres too, where people could try to find work serving a master. Among the crowds, there were plenty of opportunities for pedlars to sell their wares – or to pick a pocket or two.

How do we know? – Wage rates

Times were hard for many workers in Tudor England. The **cost of living** rose very fast, but wages did not always rise at the same rate. In Chester between 1570 and 1600 prices rose by more than 100 per cent. But in the same period, the maximum wages paid to men working there rose by only 40 per cent. This meant that people could no longer afford to buy so many things – or as much food.

Who decided what these maximum wages should be? The answer is the government in London and **Justices of the Peace** (JPs) in each 'shire' or county. By studying wage laws and reports made by JPs, we can learn a lot about Tudor jobs.

This painting by Annibale Carracci (1560–1609) shows workers in a butcher's shop. In London in 1588, a butcher's maximum wage was fixed by law at £6 per year.

London jobs in 1588

A 'proclamation' was a kind of law. It was printed, read out loud, then fixed in a public place so all could see it. One from 1588 has survived, saying what London tradesmen's wages should be. It shows us not just what jobs Tudor people did, but also how much they were meant to be paid. If the wage was high, people must have thought the trade was important. Each figure below is the maximum wage per year of 'the best and most skilful workmen' in each trade:

Clothworkers	*£5*	*Millers*	*£6*
Dyers of cloth	*£6 13s 4s*	*Saddlers*	*£4*
Tailors	*£4*	*Blacksmiths*	*£6*
Hosiers	*£4*	*Glovers*	*£3 6s 8d*
Shoemakers	*£4*	*Butchers*	*£6*
Bakers	*£3 6s 8d*	*Cooks*	*£6*
Brewers	*£10*		

In 1595, the government ordered **merchants** to raise the wages of clothworkers. These workers were given special treatment because their **industry** was so important. Cloth was, after all, England's main **export**. Even so, few clothworkers got rich. In Tudor England, almost everyone who worked with his – or her – hands had to labour hard and long for little reward.

'Money makes the world go round.' Plenty of Tudor coins have survived until today.

Timeline

1477	England's first printed book made
1485	Tudor family begins to rule over England and Wales
1492	Christopher Columbus reaches America
1513	Henry VIII leads an army to conquer France
1523	Anthony Fitzherbert's *Book of Husbandry* is published
1529–39	England stops being a Roman **Catholic** country; all the monasteries and nunneries are closed down
1538	**Parish** registers of baptisms, marriages and deaths kept from now on
1547–53	Reign of the boy-king Edward VI
1558	**Protestant** faith becomes the official faith of England
1559	Law stating that people must go to church every Sunday is passed
1563	Law passed setting new rules on **apprenticeship**, wages and work
1564–1616	Life of William Shakespeare
1577–80	Francis Drake becomes first English sea-captain to sail around the world
1585–1604	England at war with Spain
1588	English navy beats invading Spanish fleet (or Armada)
1599	The Globe Theatre opens in London
1603	End of Tudor period, as the Stuart family begins to rule

Sources and further reading

Sources
The author and Publishers gratefully acknowledge the publications from which sources in the book are drawn. In some cases the wording or sentence structure has been simplified to make the material appropriate for a school readership.

The Army of Flanders and the Spanish Road, 1567–1659, Geoffrey Parker (Cambridge University Press, 1972)

Bess of Hardwick, Kate Hubbard (Short Books, 2001)

The Common People – A History from the Norman Conquest to the Present, J.F.C. Harrison (Flamingo, 1984)

Elizabeth I and Her Reign, Ed. Richard Salter (Macmillan Documents and Debates, 1988)

Elizabethan People, Ed. Joel Hurstfield and Alan G.R. Smith (Edward Arnold Documents of Modern History, 1972)

The Elizabethan Underworld, Gamini Salgado (Alan Sutton, 1984)

The Later Tudors, Penry Williams (Oxford, 1995)

The Sixteenth Century, Patrick Collinson (Oxford, 2002)

Tudor England, 1485–1603, Ed. Roger Lockyer and Dan O'Sullivan (Longman Sources and Opinions, 1993)

The Voices of Morebath, Eamonn Duffy (Yale University Press, 2001)

Further Reading
A Tudor Kitchen, Peter Chrisp (Heinemann Library, 1997)

A Tudor School, Peter Chrisp (Heinemann Library, 1997)

Life in Tudor Times: Country Life, Jane Shuter (Heinemann Library, 1996)

Websites
www.heinemannexplore.co.uk – contains KS2 History modules including the Tudors.

www.brims.co.uk/tudors/ – information on Tudors for 7–10 year olds.

Glossary

account report or story. Also, a record of money raised and spent.

ambassador someone representing his king or queen abroad

anaesthetic pain-killer

antiseptic something to prevent spread of germs

apprentice young person learning a craft from a master

arable farmland used for growing crops

architecture the art of designing buildings

assize name of a court where criminals were put on trial

astrologer person who studies the influence of the stars on human lives

carded combed and disentangled

Catholic only Christian faith in western Europe until the 1520s, when people began to follow the Protestant faith

chaplain priest serving in a rich person's private chapel

christening church

citizen person who lives in a city

communion church service in which bread and wine are shared

cost of living prices that have to be paid for necessary things

court place where a king or queen rules from. Also, a place where criminals are tried.

courtier person who spent time at a monarch's court as a companion or adviser

dedicate devote a book or work of art to someone

export to send goods out of the country to be sold abroad

fertilize make soil richer, for farming

Flemish person who lives in Flanders (now in modern Belgium) or the language spoken there

horoscope forecast of a person's future based on the movement of planets and stars

hosiery leg-wear made by hosiers

husbandry farming, or managing a household

industry or **industrial** kind of work, other than farmwork, in which people make things

infantryman soldier who fought on foot

inventory list of a person's possessions

iron ore raw material that iron comes from

Justice of the Peace important local officials

legal to do with the law

martyr someone who dies for their religious beliefs

melancholy feeling sad

merchandise goods that are sold

merchant someone who buys and sells goods

monarch king, queen or other crowned ruler

mutton meat from a sheep

National Health Service Britain's free health-care service, started up in the mid 20th century

noblemen rich and important men who helped the monarch to run the country

Ottoman Turks Turkish people who conquered large parts of eastern Europe and Asia

parish local area with its own church and own church official

Parliament House of Lords and House of Commons, whose members met in London to advise the monarch and make laws

patron someone who supports and encourages a creative person

patronage support or encouragement given by a rich patron

Pope head of the Catholic church. He lives in Rome.

population number of people in a country

preserve stop from rotting

press machine used for printing

Protestant religious faith of people who turned away from the teachings of the Catholic church

psalm religious song or hymn

Puritan deeply committed Protestant person

Quarter Sessions courts held by Justices of the Peace

scythes tools used for cutting corn or grass

smelt to get metal out of rock by heating it up

sources books, pictures etc that give us information

sow to plant seed

taxes money paid by everyone to the monarch, to help pay for the running of the kingdom

thresh to beat corn to get the grain used to make bread

type letters or words made of metal that can be fitted together for printing

vagabonds wandering people with no fixed jobs or homes

worsted cloth made from fine wool

Index